Hair

Written by Emma Lynch

thick

thin

Hair can be thick or thin.
It can be long or short.

short

long

Hair gets longer and longer and then we get it cut.

3

We go to the hairdresser or to the barber.

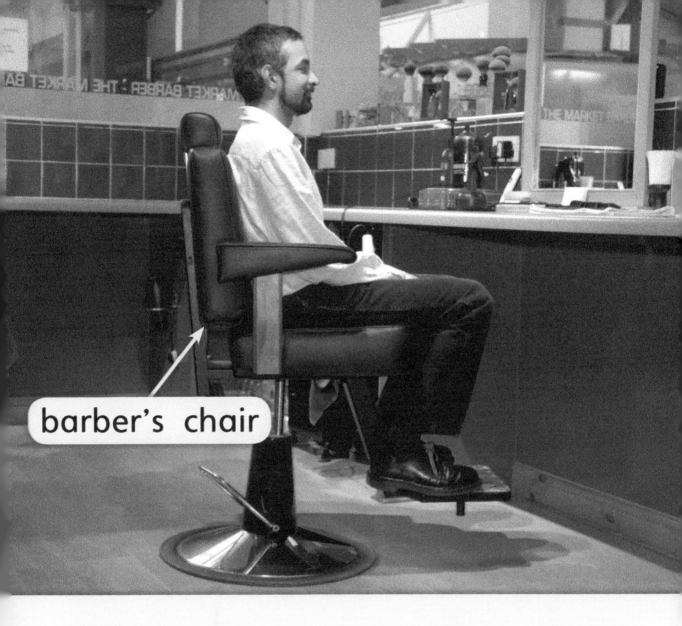

barber's chair

This man is in the barber's chair.

The barber cuts hair and beards.

brush

This brush sweeps hair from necks and ears.

The hairdresser sweeps up all the cut hair.

She has never had her hair cut.
It is long!

This is not her hair.
She has got a wig on.

This man has long hair.

This man has no hair!

turban

This man has long hair. He keeps all his hair under a turban.

Her hair was brown.

Now it is pure pink!

Long ago, men had big wigs with curls.